THE GONER SCHOOL

KUHL HOUSE POETS

Mark Levine, Lisa Wells, and Joshua Marie Wilkinson, series editors

THE GONER SCHOOL

JESSICA LASER

UNIVERSITY OF IOWA PRESS • IOWA CITY

University of Iowa Press, Iowa City 52242
Copyright © 2024 by Jessica Laser
uipress.uiowa.edu
Printed in the United States of America

Design by Nicole Hayward

Printed on acid-free paper

Library of Congress Cataloging-in-Publication Data
Names: Laser, Jessica, author.
Title: The Goner School / Jessica Laser.
Other titles: Goner School (Compilation)
Description: Iowa City: University of Iowa Press, 2024. | Series: Kuhl House Poets
Identifiers: LCCN 2024005966 (print) | LCCN 2024005967 (ebook) | ISBN
9781609389918 (paperback; acid-free paper) | ISBN 9781609389925 (ebook)
Subjects: LCGFT: Poetry.
Classification: LCC PS3612.A7884 G66 2024 (print) | LCC PS3612.A7884 (ebook) |
DDC 811/.6—dc23/eng/20240216
LC record available at https://lccn.loc.gov/2024005966
LC ebook record available at https://lccn.loc.gov/2024005967

Excerpt from *The Way of Zen* by Alan Watts, copyright © 1957 by Penguin Random
House LLC, copyright renewed 1985 by Mary Jane Watts. Used by permission of
Pantheon Books, an imprint of the Knopf Doubleday Publishing Group, a division
of Penguin Random House LLC. All rights reserved.

From "James Wright" from *Twentieth Century Pleasures* by Robert Hass. Copyright
© 1984 by Robert Hass. Used by permission of HarperCollins Publishers.

Contents

I.

Berkeley Hills Living / 3

II.

The Goner School / 13
Numbers / 16
Homework Help / 19
Fun / 22
Kings / 24

III.

Extra / 37
Thomas Jefferson / 39
William James / 41
Edward Thomas / 42
Paul Valéry / 43
The Book / 44

IV.

The Breakfast-Eaters / 49
The Afterlife / 51
Admiration / 53
Elliptical Poem / 55
Consecutive Preterite / 58

V.

Apology / 69
New Angle / 72
Parable / 73
New History / 75

I.

Berkeley Hills Living

This is not virtue in the current sense of moral rectitude but in the older sense of effectiveness, as when one speaks of the healing virtues of a plant. —ALAN WATTS

I.

Eliot's window. The glorified
hallway that served as his room.
His bed with one pillow.

Another night, it was raining too hard
to drive home and his bed had two
because a woman had visited.
Eliot and Dana talked upstairs
while I slept to the cadence
of their voices through the ceiling.
When I woke, I put on my jeans.

From his window, I could see
the eucalyptus trees' wild
gestures punctuate the fog.
The green, the gray, and nothing
beyond it. You could look at
or print or write something like it.
Something you could paint.

When I woke, I put on Lucinda Williams.
Eliot said, Aren't you happy
to spend your birthday with me?
I'll remember this with sadness, I thought,
because of what a nice moment it was:
Lucinda playing, the trees waving, tea,
but I remember it now and feel happy.

2.

Outside, the air thicker, San Francisco
blinked through the trees. Dana rolled
cigarettes on *Berkeley Hills Living*.
A couple in khakis
and cashmere graced the cover.

I was practically their neighbor, come
to earn an English PhD, for five years
of stable health insurance, to make
the two friends I did. I can honestly say
I learned nothing. Everything I learned
in California, I learned from a plant.

3.

Cameron and Ari led ceremony
at Cameron's, north of Berkeley.
You signed a waiver and, as the sun sank
over his alpacas, you drank three cups
of cactus tea, taking turns, each time you'd drink,
to pray out loud at an altar they called a highly
technical machine, able to take from you
all that you didn't need.

There was a feast after, and instruction
in the beginning, where the good

and bad news were always the same.
The good and bad news is: everyone
is innocent. The good and bad news is:
there's nothing to fix. How do you know
you're really praying? Because it's arresting.
For the writers among us, eloquence
won't be necessary. We're here
to heal, not be Dostoevsky.

4.

The English department had fashioned itself
after the kind of revelation the English department
could no longer provide. This revelation was
wrought by literature; it involved discomfort,
confusion, recognition, surprise. The department
wouldn't be moved. It got its discomfort
from critical methodology, found recognition
in new truths made of history.

But ceremony had already taught me
something about history I couldn't forget:
everyone messing each other up—they
were all just doing their best. My ancestors
did more than flee the Tsar, sell used clothes
on Maxwell Street. The whole time, they were
praying me into being. That I live
is the sign of their success.

5.

Cameron led meditation
from the altar in the center of the circle.
The waning daylight made my eyelids gauze
it could shine through. Think of a time
you felt unconditionally loved, he said.

It doesn't matter who. We spent time
living in that memory and I wept
the California light back out of my eyes.
I had sudden, irrevocable access
to so much love, I thought I might die.

That was how ceremony
taught you to be happy.
Before, you thought all
happiness was conditional.

6.

I couldn't eat. I leaned against a counter,
asked Max if he remembered
something we once did together
with olive oil. He showed me a picture
of his children. Someone passed me
bread and I was asked to slice it.
I don't know where a knife is.
I took a knife out of the indicated drawer.
I don't hate the program, I told Michael,
who'd asked. It's something I've chosen.
Then Michael came up to ask about the program.
I don't hate it, I said. I just have to figure out how
to be better. How's yours?
OK, he said. I'm ABD.
Wow, I said. The bread pure texture,
the knife pure control, I lamented privately
that I was done cutting it. Tyler was stirring
the soup I'd been asked to provide.
I brought that, I said.
Nice, he said.
Yeah, I said. Then to Michael,
I just have to figure out what I want.

It's not in the books, Michael said.
Yeah, I said. Then I added,
Maybe not for you.

7.

I am done cutting this bread,
I announced. Someone arrived
with a basket. Eve. She took the knife
from my hand and put it in the sink.
I stirred soup and focused
on the aromatics of the steam.
Isn't it funny? In a way,
it seemed like sex to me, sex with life,
breath moving in and out of my body,
the most unconditional love I'd had.

Another night, I'd stood over a flame,
asked Dana and Eliot which courses
I should take. Eliot said I'd phrased it
in an odd way, a moral register.
I'd asked if taking such courses
would be ill-advised. He told me
I was obsessed with morality.
Dana came as ever to my rescue,
telling Eliot that he, in fact, was obsessed
with morality, for having characterized
my neutral question as moral.

In the center, we offered
a last prayer before breaking our fast.
Max shifted uncomfortably, or maybe
it was me. He had been in recovery,
surfing. I'd lie out on his giant beach towel
reading Stevens, taking and then sending

videos to my friends. One video included
my breasts and "Sailing After Lunch."

omg

omg

im so sorry,

Eric wrote me. He had accidentally
forwarded it to Chris.

8.

I had started with some silly words
I don't remember now, felt
watched and embarrassed, until I said
I guess the bottom line
is that I would like to fall in love with my life.

I hugged Cameron on the way back to my seat.
His wife usually joined for ceremony, but that afternoon
she was pregnant with their baby. Cameron's prayers
were always about her, about being more
of what makes her happy. When we hugged, he said
That's what I want, too.

9.

I had wanted to get to the bottom line.
There were so many people in the circle,
it seemed important not to take up time.
But I would get up and offer my prayer
and sit back down and think of important things
I hadn't said. And then I wondered if I shouldn't
go back up and say them. It can't be, I consoled myself,

that only prayers offered at this altar are answered.
But I had never asked for more medicine than the minimum,
and it seemed time to try something new. So I interrupted,
it was just before Eve's turn, and said, Eve, is this OK?
And she was so obliging then, like a mother.

10.

In the next room, two couches faced each other.
The floor to ceiling windows revealed a huge
and terrifying external darkness. Cameron
was eating a plate of steak and chicken
and quinoa with currants and pizza and salad
on one of the couches, talking to someone
he knew, beside him, who was also eating
though with less vitality. I listened to them talk
about buying property in Hawaii.

11.

I first heard of chakras in a physical theater
intensive I took one summer in college.
The teacher played vaguely tribal music
while we explored them one by one, starting
with the red one at the base of the pelvis,
not touching that area but moving from it,
featuring it as the movement's driving force.

As sometimes happened, I started crying
and had to leave the room. That's how I met Sonya
who introduced me to Max when I lived with her
after college in Topanga. We lay semi-supine
in the hallway outside of our classroom.
Are you OK? she asked after a while. Yeah,
I said. OK, she said, then I'm going back in.

When I went back in, I expected the teacher
to congratulate me on the depth of my feeling.
Instead she said, These are techniques
you are learning for the sake of the theater. It's
as important that you are able to inhabit a moment
as it is that you are able to move on from it
completely, without a trace.

12.

Eliot touched my face and told me
I would live into my nineties.
I ate some cream of mushroom
soup Eve made. Michael drove home
while I navigated, reciting all the poems
I'd ever known to stay awake.
He had to pull over more than once
so I could do something Cameron
and Ari called "get well." I must have been
holding onto ceremony, I thought, bending
over a grate on the side of the highway,
because here I am letting it go.

II.

The Goner School

We did dangerous and stupid things
Were dangerous and stupid
Ignorant and arrogant
We did things we saw people do

Saved by what we didn't know
Could happen

We were just getting young
Caught dangerous and stupid
With our educations written all over us
Our huge, expensive educations

We were so caught up
In danger and stupidity
With our big, empty eyes
Our stupid, heavily lined eyes
Our energies, eyes with the stakes
Emptied out of them
Night diner fluorescence
Our youth was caught
In the glare of

I had a hot chocolate
The boys had omelets

You could dim us

We wept and fasted, wept
And prayed and our periods came

Actually, we were pregnant

We had sex like a dictionary

We wanted to be other
For others were better
Than we were to ourselves

With our stupid eyes and bigger mouths
We were pregnant with ourselves

In the Water Tower
At the makeup counter
We were bitchy and hungry
And blamed other women
Our youth caught in their glare

By pissy trucks and passing grain
We drove dangerously, stupidly
Unto passing trucks who honked
We did danger and left nothing out

Sun caught their windshields
As we passed, speeding
Each toward more Midwest
A place I didn't know
I was from

Until trees spit moss
And Shasta loomed
And hot springs waited
For the time we'd go

I always said what kind of person I was
I was that kind of person

Numbers

The premise was I'd never done anything
like this. My portion was Moses
and the Cushite woman. I delivered some words
on racism. Miriam and Aaron didn't accept her
because she was darker than they were. Is Judaism
religion or ethnicity? Which number wife
of Moses was she? The chapel, not the synagogue.
The synagogue, not the temple. In Numbers,
Miriam and Aaron, Moses's siblings,
speak against his marriage and that's how
we find out he's married her.
Where was the love story? Enemies,
family, crushes, members of the
KAM Isaiah Israel congregation,
I ask you now whether this is a story
about leaving the love story out
because other kinds of stories merit
inclusion, stories about enslavement
and liberation, acceptance by and of
one's family, rage that prevents
the transmission of the sacred, rage
that excludes from within. Those
were the days god spoke to my people
face to face, before his promise became
no miracles. That explains it.

You're four miles from me and still
we won't see each other.
There are roads, cars, the notion
of transportation, but we are forever
here and now, statues of ourselves,
golden calves our souls worship
into flesh until Moses comes down
and marries a Cushite woman, breaking
with his characteristic rage. All our law
is already revision. Who first thought
of movement? The wind? The leaf
fluttering on a tree whose bark
wasn't thinking? I think of you
and imagine speeds beyond anything
just a little faster, just to run my finger
along your palm, the centuries there,
in the smell of your hair. Sometimes,
lord knows, we have these
satisfactions so complete
they don't fit, mar the texture of our
fleece-lined lives. No one talks
about the trauma pleasure is
except Bob Hass, who in the seventies
described it as something to survive.
In those, the days of miracles, there was
a lot of gathering, peoples whose fates then
forked like roads in the wood where roads
were invented, the second line a botched
emphasis on the first, set off just a bit
to the side. Then god took his happy
error and invented perpendicularity
and there was intersection, like Moses
and the Cushite woman. This
shall be a road, said the creator,
a line and another, for those who
come go away. Where roads are

there will be no staying, only
lingering to glean one's wintry wisdom
from the sound the snow makes when it falls
on harness bells that still shake.
When Miriam spoke against the Cushite woman,
god made her "white as snow." To Moses,
god would make himself known
in his "similitude." This passage
is also about god. Let a prophet
come forth: I'll speak to him
in a dream. But Moses he will speak with
mouth to mouth. Moses, reluctant
prophet of the waking hours, escape
from bondage, the dreamless sleep,
sutured to wonder, sentenced
to wander, to lead his people to gates
he would not enter. I too would have
struck that stone, would have hit
with my staff the stone meant miraculously
to give water. A stone giving water
in a desert I was not born to enter
unto a thirst I did nothing to deserve
would not appease my anger
at the enslavement of my people.
Water from a stone, from a stone
I would strike, and god forbid
I had a gun. What wouldn't I
use it on? Miracles? I am created
in the image of an angry,
jealous god I call my own.
My love is as exclusive as my god.
I save it for the Cushite woman,
her only, in the age of polygamy.

Homework Help

Impersonal grows from personal love, the cooling breeding,
in place of obsession, attention that seeks virtue and wisdom
and sees the loved object as means to those things.
Jason, the high school junior assigned to me, with the daughter
of the owner of the vineyard was in love. Because his parents
liked his progress, my volunteer gig had turned with the season
to paid summer tutoring during which Jason confided in me
and completed assignments I devised. Because he was in love
I had asked him to write a brief essay relating Denis Johnson's
"Car Crash While Hitchhiking" to Ralph Waldo Emerson's "Love."
In his first draft, he had tried to prove that the salesman driver,
a minor character, the first of four to pick up the hitchhiker,
in being, as Johnson says, "gifted with love," in loving his wife,
kids, girlfriend, relatives, boat, two cars, and backyard
had, in Emerson's terms, supplanted relation after relation
"only by what is more beautiful." Errors in speech point
to errors in thinking, and I asked Jason to consider that
in his thesis there might be a grammatical one. "Was it in where I said,
'Johnson's protagonist is a drug addict'?" he asked. "Why would it
be in that sentence?" I said. "I don't know," said Jason.
"Should it just say he's addicted to drugs?" "I'll give you a hint,"
I said. "It's a preposition." "Remind me," said Jason,
"what a preposition is." "Over under through with by," said I.
Jason looked over his paper, at me, then over his paper again.
I pointed to a region on the page. "Oh—" he said, "I said that

the salesman supplants the relations 'by' when I should have said 'with.'"
We high-fived. "So how," I asked, "does that reveal a larger problem?"
Jason then acted on an instinct I love, which was to retrieve
from his backpack the Emerson essay and find in the original
the disputed quote. "He says, 'That which is so beautiful and
attractive as these relations must be succeeded and supplanted
only by what is more beautiful, and so on forever.'" "OK,"
I said, "who supplants in your thesis?" "The salesman," said Jason.
"Who supplants in the Emerson?" Jason reread the quote a few times.
"No one," he said. "The relations just are supplanted by each other,
it's like they don't really supplant." "That's passive voice," I said,
"and Emerson is using it to speak of the natural course of things,
how love progresses without will, just by letting beauty have its way."
"Oh," said Jason, "so I can't say the salesman supplants his wife
with his girlfriend—or I can, but that's not what Emerson means?"
"Exactly," I said. "So what do I do?" "You revise your essay
for next week." Jason sighed and gave me a look that meant
my devices were working on him, but still he was forced
by his parents to attend summer tutoring that life would be better,
be simpler without. Others might call this an eye roll. I laughed,
and teased, "Have fun with Molly." "Molly goes to camp this week."
"Oh no!" I said. "Yeah," he said, "life is over." "May as well
write a good essay," I said. "That's what we do when life ends."
A lot of what I told him we both hoped he'd understand
later, when he was a little older. His mom honked in the Saab.
She held up to the window a sandwich in a Ziploc. "Tuna," said Jason.
"I'm going to a music lesson." "Why don't they let you off the hook
once in a while?" "They will," said Jason. "I get August off
for camp." "Have you ever done nothing or had nothing to do?"
"No," he said, "but I have been bored." Sometimes it seemed like
the library door remained completely open once he'd left
and I'd finish the parts of the crossword I could do, until a huge
wind blew the paper away and slowly, over many Thursdays,
the library filled past recognition with my papers, blown
against the far wall like a dune. I'd browse the DVDs,
text Meg to see if she wanted anything, then stop by

the IGA on my way home. Life couldn't have been more
normal seeming, and yet I felt like I had no family,
felt far away from being known. On Friday nights,
the library showed cult classics at 11. Once I saw Jason
and Molly on a Friday, driving his mom's Saab away
from the library. Goodbye, I thought and said quietly, Goodbye
young lovers, good day, goodbye, my heart goes with you, my soul
and my body—as if to them I had relinquished all
memory of love, as if I had to learn it all again.
The movie had been *Trollhunter* and I had fallen asleep, Meg
beside me eating Twizzlers. She hadn't been drinking and then
she started up again. Her eyes would bug out and she'd open my door
to tell me she was in love with me, that I was the most beautiful
woman she'd seen. Meg, I'd say, it's time to go to sleep, but she'd
say no and weep in my arms, and we would talk about her family.
I was so into the idea that we knew each other fully
I couldn't see I knew nothing of her. She felt like a sister
but wasn't familiar to me. I didn't know how different
other people could be, that my upbringing shaped my expectation
of friendship, hers shaped hers differently, and by these
expectations we were led blindly, laid down and swaddled.
Amazingly, despite what I just said, I still believe nothing
ensures a happy adult like the child's perseverance.

Fun

Chocomania
Chocolate Peanut Butter
Grasshopper
Yellow Cake Batter

The final hill to climb will be a dune
The oceans lick from either side
Crowding the center
Is there ivy on the dune?

Dune grass
Is there a bathing suit?
Air conditioning
You put on cold

And greasy sunscreen
Beyond the dune I remember nothing
Must have been carried there, final hill
Indiana

From the beach you can see it
Emit its huge white pillar of steam
Oceans are scary
Waves in the lake on a rainy day

Body full of stones
Some round, some smooth, some pretty
Some heart-shaped
I was good at collapsing them

And ping-pong
We bought the neighbor's house
Made me as pretty as their daughter
Tim knocking there summer after summer

College Tim, bulked up, a gold chain
High school Tim, cargo shorts and gray Hanes
This is what it costs to keep these houses up
We live at 7

The trolley was retired, leaving the stops
Chocomania
Chocolate Peanut Butter
Grasshopper

Why didn't you warn me? I asked
My mother the summer
Oink's had suddenly changed all their ice cream
Maybe it will be even better now, she said

What are things that merit mourning?
Beach chair
Water catching lightning
Watching the storm from inside

Kings

I.

Kings lie down to zip up their jeans,
buy Cetaphil, candy, magazines
at Walgreens because they can
walk there unsupervised, describe
blow jobs they've given to seniors
in cars, spend what they think of as
their own money. Home sick from school,
they learn about G-strings from daytime TV.
A *Jerry Springer* episode: "My Daughter
Dresses Like a Ho!" and a mom comes on
waving a finger at a whooping audience
who quiets as she opens a variety pack
Band-Aid box out of which she pulls her
daughter's clothes.

We named those thongs for this one
beautiful junior who, in the cafeteria,
sat down within view. Why it was
we had to be in high school
at the same time an extremely lowriding
jeans trend arose, we'll never know.

2.

Kristen went to Catholic school
so everyone had already been kissed.
As a girl, that's how you made it
to first base. You didn't kiss
you were kissed. What does it mean
to get fingered? I asked her, the term itself
insufficiently illustrative. She made a motion.
My eyes widened. "It's really
more for the guy," she said.

People got fingered on the beach
and drank beer. For dinner, we ordered
Little Giant. I was kissed
by a friend of hers who later said
I was an airhead. At Walgreens,
I bought candy to bring to Michigan City.
It's amazing that we did
what we did among the very sandcastles
of our youth. There he was by the dune.
"Hey," he said. But I just handed him
an Airhead and went to swim.

3.

That was all we were doing: playing Kings.
There's a can of beer in the center and cards
fanned out around it, or a Solo cup full of
whatever people pour in. Each card means a different
collective activity, rhyming or raising a hand.
If you're last or you can't rhyme, you drink.
Sometimes it's a "social" and everyone
drinks together. The goal is to get drunk,
even though that means losing. Fives were guys,
sixes chicks. In the strip version, those cards indicated

collective stripping by gender. You never knew
whether it would be strip or not, so you always
considered wearing layers. It was summer.
Sometimes you'd get pretty naked
but it wasn't pushy. You could take off
one sock at a time.

4.

Which boy's feet you sat at mattered.
Strip Kings or not, the feet determined
the course of your night. I sat at Tim's.

I went upstairs for a drink when he did.
We paused in the hallway, his breath,
his skin, deodorant, laundry detergent.

He stepped back to look at me
and shook his head, marveling
at the strength of our restraint.

"That's just what he's like
with girls from out of town,"
Kristen kept saying.

5.

Andrew was my ride
from the North Side some mornings.
It was navy blue, his minivan, someone
in the family's discarded car. He blasted
dry, minimal Chicago hip-hop
and we made out at stoplights
but I was in love with Matt.

Matt and I lay in bed for hours
listening to *The Rhythm of the Saints*
and showered at his dad's when
only his stepmom was home.

We sat on the couch. I tried, watching him
play *Grand Theft Auto*, to be supportive,
to comment on the game's genius
design and look generally
interested and skinny.

Matt left the room right after he told me
he was getting back with Kim.
He came back in with a paper towel
taped to his shoulder, opened his arms
and grinned like you can laugh
even while you cry on me.
I didn't move toward him.

6.

Sam and Matt had been good friends,
co-captains of the soccer team. I don't
remember why they fell out. How it started
between us was Sam kept asking me
to walk to 57th Street for lunch.
He never believed that stuff
I did with him I hadn't done with Matt,
but I hadn't, not with anyone.
He turned 18 and I gave him
an original *Pulp Fiction* movie poster.

"Can't we just ride out the summer?"
We were breaking up for college.
No, I said, having left my body
upstairs in a distant hallway.

I think we should start the process now.
"I pressured you to have sex," he said.
"You shouldn't have lost it to me."

I was just as bad
as his other ex-girlfriend.
She was actually a popular hot girl,
not a might-be-hot-in-a-few-years
type guys could feel they'd plucked
from innocence, like me.

"Turns out you're just like her,"
he said. Maybe I'd wanted that
from being his girlfriend. Maybe
she was what I'd wanted to be.

7.

I pulled into St. Joe around two
and felt giddy. I met Tim, already
dressed for the wedding,
coming out of the elevator,
his suit sleeve just hinting
at a bicep beneath.

He stared like I didn't know
you were going to be here.
"What's your room number?"
308. The knock came. Kristen
didn't tell you? It was her wedding.
"No," he said, lifting my dress.

8.

He called drunk from his dad's
sometimes at 2 or 3 a.m., a number

I'd learned by heart at seventeen. I'd lie in bed
and watch the call come in. So this is what I am,
I said to myself, his girlfriend calling my room
twice the night of the wedding. I haven't
seen him, I haven't seen him, I said.

He said he'd spent the earlier part of the day
beating in the face of a guy who sold drugs
to his mom. He showed me his hands
but the knuckles weren't bruised. I couldn't tell
if the drinks had made him confuse
fantasy and reality, just like I couldn't
in my hotel room tell whether I had confused
the same thing. Tim, I said, why
are we doing this? "Because," he said,
"this is what we do."

9.

The man with the NRA hat and I
had, on the trail, a pleasant exchange.
"We're from Indiana," his wife said.
I'm from Chicago, I said.
"We're from southern Indiana," he said.
I see. As I walked away,
I thought about his hat.

What could I say about guns?
I don't know if I should, if
I shot one. There was a ranch.
I was in school. Elementary.
We were going to shoot cans
but my leg went into the frozen
lake instead. I screamed
and we had to go home.
It was winter, summer,

29

hunting season. It was is that
a gun? Fireworks we watched
from Laurie's roof, not a boat we'd taken
out on the lake. I think I'm between
a boat and a lake when I think
somebody owns that boat, nobody
this lake. I will be owned by the ground
I walk on, kept by the air I breathe.

10.

An article appeared in my newsfeed.
Michigan City Man Airlifted to South Bend
Bleeding from Skull. Hadn't the ranch
been there, where my leg went
through the ice? "Love you, Tim,"
the comment read. I'd felt so good
picking up and telling him
he was drunk and I wasn't
available, or letting the call
go to voicemail, waking up,
seeing it and not calling
back. Dear everyone
I loved and never told,
I loved Tim and never told him.

11.

I did tell him once, in my kitchen.
He'd said it first, so I was safe.
I told him I'd marry him. "You'd
marry me?" We were drinking
martinis. He was in a relationship
with someone with my name.
Yeah, I'd marry you, I said.
"But aren't you slumming it right now?"

He grew up where my family
had a second home. His dad's
was just down the road.
He'd come for me barefoot
in a three-wheeled golf cart,
his drink on what would have been
the dash.

Do you ever think about actually
being with me? I should have said
in bed, in the basement, the shower,
on the beach at dawn. But he was
in college and I wasn't anything
like the girlfriends he brought home.
I don't feel that I'm slumming it
with you, no, I said. He sipped
his martini. "Damn," he said,
"I always thought that maybe
I could have a different life."

12.

We walked from mine
to his dad's. I followed him down
to where I used to sit at his feet.
He wanted to show me something,
which turned out to be a rifle
he pointed at me. Put the gun down,
Brad, I thought, reciting a line
from a scene I'd once studied.
Daniel, my scene partner,
was Brad. "I just want to get a look
at the little lady," his line said next.

The class was amazing. We did
exercises that didn't resemble reality

in order to make our scenes more real.
In one exercise, each partner held
the end of a rope. Delivering a line
meant manipulating the rope in some way,
pulling, yanking, wrapping, knotting,
tying oneself or someone else up.
This permitted the surfacing and physical
expression of hidden motivations,
as when the other Jess and Peter,
her scene partner, found themselves
completely wrapped up together, him
behind her, the rope so tangled you'd
sooner step out of than unwrap it,
while their characters, exes who'd run
into each other in line for the bathroom
of a restaurant they'd attended on dates
with other people, spoke about fondue.

Another exercise had us move
freely through the fully fleshed out
details of our set, to try to defamiliarize
things like tables and chairs, glasses
and guns, floors, even, and ceilings,
to try, in our scenes, to employ those things
in a more human way. You'd be surprised
how much work it takes to approximate
human beings onstage, even when
you are one. Most actors just pick up
a glass and drink, but god knows a glass
is for running one's finger along
the rim of, spilling, moving from one
side of a table to the other, passing
to a friend for a sip. The glass,
in this sense, is another scene partner,
in relation to whom a whole human
drama unfolds. Actors think

a gun, I know what this is, this
is how a person holds a gun, or
a kitchen, I know what this is,
this is how a person is in a kitchen,
but god knows the running joke had been
Cooper smoking pot while I made eyes
at Tim, me saying, Please, Cooper,
don't do that in my kitchen and him
saying, and everyone repeating for years,
"Wait, I'm in your kitchen?"

When Daniel had the gun,
that time we moved freely, he wasn't
pointing it at me so much as lifting me up
who was draped over its barrel. Put it down,
I insisted. "I just want to get a look," he said.
We were divorcing. I was taking our sons
to Portland. My name was Colleen.

13.

Tim showing me the coat of arms
newly installed on his shoulder blade.
"My sister got one, too," he said. "It's a family
crest. See? Here's my Irish side, here's
my American side." He vaguely touched
his back as he spoke. You have to get better
at pointing them out, I said.
"Show me," he said, guiding my hand.
"Here are the books. Here are the dogs."
No, I said, they're here and they're here.

14.

Tim hit a curb, riding
his motorcycle. Now, though

his tattoo's intact, his brain
will never be the same.

I think this must be what love is.
You tend a little fire that is someone
in your system, and even though
the facts might point in one direction,
out, you go on tending it
because that is what you do.

III.

Extra

I breathe and the I
Love and the I
Am and the I
Is extra

I held father's hand
Smelled mother's perfume
In eucalyptus after rain
You could find me

Enveloped in your arms
Hot breath, a vital, portable
Part of you stays, part of me
That goes with you

In winter, in summer
Disappointed and happy
With my body in pain
And the soothing of pain

Times I believed I could change
The world, times I believed
I was extra
I wore clothes and read books

I could have hated, chose
Not to and there was no I
My heart, my lungs
Legs, hands, and liver

Held me indistinctly
A member of groups
Nothing unique
About my experience

For I had not valued uniqueness
For I had not considered
Uniqueness required
For my experience to be valuable

Thomas Jefferson

I said I was a horse
because I like to be compelled.

You said it when you called
adulthood learning
to live according to your values.

Could you have a value
that says it is my value
to have values that do not conflict?

A horse just carries
obedience gracefully,
like that one choice you made
without deliberating.

Thomas Jefferson invented
the swivel chair, apparently
desiring to build all sides
of an argument into a piece
of furniture, and even if,
with that reading, I wouldn't
at first agree, I could see
swiveling my way there.

I said I was a horse but
of course I was a chair.

And the chair I was is the horse
I will be, that's how I get
all the legs I need.

Who hasn't once or twice
said the wrong thing?
Who hasn't said something right?

Sometimes the right words lag
behind you, and you are their horse
for a season, for a season
you are their transportation.

William James

As I enter the station, my first heart stops.
I begin, chopping the foot of a tree.
Its branches are unmoved by my act.
Its leaves murmur. Peacefully as ever,
I do violence to the foot of a man.
I hear the conductor calling "all aboard!"
If I stumble as I run
If a cinder enters my eye

I enter the station.
The conductor calling "all aboard!"
Stops my first heart stopping
My second heart beating
The foot of a tree, the foot
Of a man. I hear violence calling
Its branches unmoved.
They are moved, I insist.

Edward Thomas

Sometimes I read you for anger
To see in your face

The confines of a medium.
What wouldn't I think

To be a thought in your head?
The youngest and most beautiful

Love no one, but still I love
Everyone I've loved.

"I love roads"

Unlike a governmental body,
Mine can be shot

In the street in the broad
Daylight of democracy.

I'd leave this country
But democracy loves me.

Paul Valéry

Forced, I chose the literature of America
Over England, figuring I'd never understand why
The Countess caught the 8 o'clock train

And not the 7, finding a certain esoterica
In the thinking of those whose aristocratic titles buy
Them out of stooping to the literature of America

When you grow up here, in the Midwest
Your imagination narrows to the private jets of celebrity
Never the 8 o'clock trains of countesses

For this is what it is to be a Jessica
Just another early decision applicant to the Ivies
Intending, if major she must, to study the literature of America

Why is life so disappointing? Sometimes with a flicker
Of fulfillment, some moving moment in a book, the cry
Of the 8 o'clock train pulling away

We'd spoken in the dining car, even bickered,
Debating the merits of nationalizing any literature
When she left us, the Countess, on the 8 o'clock train
To carve from talk a literature of our own

The Book

I pulled out the book in horror
I thought the book the one
I meant to leave you after dinner
That in my haste I must have taken it
With me with my things

When I got home it was another
One you hadn't given me
That felt to my hand like one I'd give you
Back but with a different cover

Small tight book
In which we write our failure, submission
Such a violent book

That's when I get by
A girl, guided by one
To a rhinestone

She pulls out a mirror
She knows what violences are

I put her book inside my book to save my place

Between my real lives
I loved to live this one
Safe beneath the symptom
Shaded by the sycamore
More word than tree

IV.

The Breakfast-Eaters

These two sunny-side up eggs on my plate
are the eyes of a god who stares back.
And the small bouquet in the center's glass vase,
sugar packets, silver metal creamer, people refilling
your decaf, regular, wondering, wondering
all the same thing. How does life begin again?
Did my life begin? And when? The tombs
we build in books in rooms in clouds, the tombs
we build of stuff in our house, dogs we've loved,
people we've learned to, who share blood,
passions, colleagues, who happen upon us
each day in the street. I bumped into one
turning from kissing someone to leave. I said
I was sorry. I said I was sorry! She seemed
not to want to forgive me. Was that when
my life began? Poached eggs on a ciabatta bun
with avocado subbed for bacon, herbed mayo
and tomato jam. Was that when?

Life is a broken fast
broken fast. We must fortify
against it, first thing in the morning.
Oh you, who think the day another
tray returned delicious to the bin,
coffee refill station you visit once

you've exhausted, for staying awake,
all your first plans, know that I am only tired when
I've merited the slackening of my energies.
I'll sleep but not because it's night.
I'll sleep because I've done enough.
And when I wake, it will be time
that's pulled those energies taut
to leak them out slowly toward sleep.

The Afterlife

I could take out the recycling
and die if I don't
run into him. I could sit
in the garden and die
if he doesn't walk by.

I am in love with my neighbor.
Is it obvious
a pandemic rages,
that we've all
been stuck inside?

My neighbor is a professional.
He rides his motorcycle
to fly big jets. I hear him leave
from my bed. From my couch,
I hear him come back. He's

too sexy to get furloughed.
The airlines would miss him,
they'd fold. Last night,
he taught me to disarm
his gun. I do love a man

whose priority is safety
but I think I'll die anyway:
the long, slow, excruciating
death of wondering if today
he's forgotten about me.

Once I was not living but merely
surviving. Now I am not
surviving at all. I read in a book
The worst has already happened
but when he comes home

I forget all my plans. I think I intended
to shower. Shall I crawl there?
I am in love with my neighbor.
I'll die if he doesn't
text back. He'll come home

and I'll know, or he won't
and then, O misery, where
would he be? I'd be here,
dying of guessing, listening
to *Lover* by Taylor Swift.

In one song, she thought
something would kill her
but it didn't. I felt
a little sorry for her.
You should have let it, Taylor!

Let me rewrite your song.
You thought that it would kill you
and it did. You're singing this
from the afterlife, where only
those brave enough to live die.

Admiration

We fought so hard Teddy told me
to pull over on the highway so he could get out.
Why pop musicians use children's voices
in their songs was what we were fighting about.
I asked him why he thought they did.
"Huh," he said, "I never thought about that."
"You never thought about that?" I asked, really asking
"Why haven't you ever thought about anything?"
and really saying, "You've been all your life
so talented and beautiful you've never had to
think." He almost moved to Iowa with me.
Instead, from our collective existence blessed
by natural gifts erupted miseries we are still kept
apart and from our better labors by. Teddy's
disregard for health and even sometimes
life itself inspires me. He could do anything
but likes to fail, so though his presence
creates expectation, no one expects of him
more than he's willing to give. He saves the time
he doesn't spend for the musician he will be
or is, as I suspect we have by now become
what we always thought we were
working toward. Teddy made me feel
I could do anything. He told me
if I'd picked up the cello young enough

I'd have been better than him.
That's a picture of our love then,
mine usurped by Teddy's obsession,
the healthy part of which, his admiration,
changed me irreversibly. Now Teddy
admires no one, which is the first step
toward real humility. "Of course
I think I'm better than you," he said to
but not of me. He said it as part of a story.
We had been walking with sweating iced teas
but stopped to sit on the small side steps of
the Ukrainian Catholic Church with gold mosaics.
He described his latest breakup and breaking in
to his ex's house to steal back the mandolin
she stole from him. With me, he never even
got out of the car. Teddy had a white van
that smelled like Serenity, an essential oil blend
"someone gave me" and that before the ride
home he applied to my wrists and neck.
"I just think that if anything happens
between us again it should be with intention,"
I said. Teddy laughed. "I understand," he said,
"why you would say that." We pulled up
outside the Meter Building, on Wood Street,
where once, when I was asleep and didn't hear
the landline ring, he left a note on my car
that read, "I'm on our side."
We go on faith that others know
the silent contracts we keep with them.
It was of Teddy my misconception
that to the unspoken he lacked
the subtlety to agree. It was my own
lack of subtlety I couldn't see.
Leaving the van, I turned to make sure
I hadn't left anything in my seat.

Elliptical Poem

I loved even evenings
snow covered the ground
and I would bundle
my way out, my wet hair
tucked in a scarf.

I loved showering there,
the astringent foaming soap
from the wall dispenser, meant to serve
as shampoo and conditioner.

We met at the gym
or made plans to meet.
It was where we worked out.

We'd take the high table
across from the desk.
I'd have slowly stretched
while you finished your exorbitant
visit to the elliptical.

We'd drink water
and stare at each other.

It made the gym
a place of wonder.

For thirty minutes, I'd watch people
enter the aerobics room, alone
or in twos, then move in unison.

The aerobics class required dumbbells
and some people brought their own,
purple or pink, hunter or aqua, each
five pounds or one pound or three.

I used a machine of which
there were only a few
and a crew of us knew
each other, who used them,
especially an old man
with a terrycloth sweatband
and me. We gave each other
nods of greeting, acknowledging
our familiarity and shared love
of the machine. We did so
in headphones, without speaking.

You'd be on a different machine
in a row behind us, sweating.

I liked that
I couldn't see you
but you could see me.

I listened to long songs,
eleven minutes, thirteen,
to make the thirty pass more quickly.

I did pigeon in the stretch area
with shiny blonde wood.
From there, I could see you
but don't remember trying to.

When you weren't coming,
I'd go to a class.

Once we hadn't planned to meet
when from my machine
I saw you exit spin. I never thought
it was your duty to me
to say you'd be at the gym
but you looked for me,
coming out of that room,
as after classes I had looked for you.

You must have been playing
a game with yourself
where you got to see me
and pretend you weren't trying to.

My classes weren't in the aerobics room
but another, to the left, one with a mirror
and, along it, a bar. There I did things
resembling circuit training.

I loved showering at the gym
because it was winter. At home,
I'd stand naked and freezing, waiting
for the water to heat, but there
the water heated faster and besides,
I was already warm.

Consecutive Preterite

I.

That summer I learned biblical Hebrew
with Christian women jerking themselves
toward ministry one brick building at a time.
We got along well, they and I and our teacher,
a religious studies graduate student who spent
eight hours a day transmitting the grammar
and syntactical rules of ancient languages,
afternoons training one student in Ethiopic,
mornings with the six of us.

Biblical Hebrew conveys meaning
through roots, he taught us. Each root
consists of three consonants. OK.
Some roots appear the same but differ
in meaning or pronunciation. Oh no,
we groaned. Things were getting complicated.
The meanings we'd have to look up
in our Brown-Driver-Briggs lexicons;
the pronunciations we'd learn to recognize
thanks to a vowel system long ago standardized
from the Masoretic text. When will you teach us
how to look things up? one of us asked.
The rest of us cooed. The teacher must have said later
or soon. It was a fast-moving intensive.

I'd neglected to bring my lexicon to class,
it was too heavy, and to tell the truth, I had
not once opened it since it arrived
addressed to a former lover from whom
that summer I was subletting.
I had addressed it that way so as to avoid
confusion, that of the mail personnel.
I had not considered that it might not function
like a regular English dictionary. English
words you look up by first letter,
but these you could only find after
you'd learned to read them for roots.

2.

At an unknown point in the deliberations
by committee that led to the King James
translation of the Bible in the early seventeenth
century, someone had the brilliant idea
to distinguish between English words
with exact equivalents in the "Originall tongues"
and those without direct corollary. This is why,
even in contemporary printings, the translation is full
of italics, marking words with which the translators
were forced to supplement original text
in order to make their translation make sense
to a humanity so fallen as to be English-speaking,
an English-speaking humanity. It wasn't that
previous translators, of which there weren't,
as there are now, excessive numbers, had found
a way to translate more perfectly, only
that the King James translators were first
to acknowledge in print the inconvenience,
and also their reluctance to interpolate at all
at a time when translation had only recently

distinguished itself legally from blasphemy
and punishment for blasphemy was death.

The habit of italicizing added words came
with first quarto and octavo editions, printed
for small churches or private use in 1612.
Robert Barker, King James's troubled,
bankrupt royal printer, used roman type
for these throughout and italicized words
he'd previously had in roman in the 1611
first folio editions, now called "He" and "She"
bibles, demarcating what appear to have been
two first printings, Ruth 3:15 the key difference
between them, where, having slept at his feet
on the threshing room floor, Ruth brings Boaz
a garment he's asked for, and he empties
six measures of barley into it. Then one of them
goes into the city, he or she, Boaz with the barley,
Ruth with the barley, or Boaz alone while Ruth
takes the barley elsewhere. Another verse has Ruth
showing barley to Naomi. Still, someone
went into the city, and it could have been Ruth
bringing Naomi the barley, or Boaz on other business.

3.

If some words are closer to God, and these are those
that can be translated directly, if all languages
share a source their words in common evince
the most minimal human intervention in,
then what does it mean that biblical Hebrew
lacks a word that directly approximates *is*?

Italics in the King James translation
seem always to emphasize states of being,

as if in the speaker, a transformation has occurred
just prior to the act of speaking, making the speech
describe a past that no longer holds true. A good
example of this is Psalm 73:16—"When I thought
to know this, it *was* too painful for me."

4.

Biblical Hebrew, our teacher said,
has a tense reserved for narrative.
He called it "consecutive preterite."
It marks events that transpired in the past,
successively. You make it by putting
the word *and* before a jussive. Does
anyone know what a jussive is?
No one said yes. A jussive
is a kind of prayerful thinking. Instead
of "he ran," you'd say, "may he run,"
or "let him." Oh wow, I said,
has anyone heard of Christopher Smart?

After a few days, or their equivalent
in weeks, I went home and tried reading.
I opened my brown, leather-bound
Biblia Hebraica to Genesis, in Hebrew
named for its first word, a compound
equivalent to multiple words in translation:
In the Beginning. I liked imagining other
books retitled this way: *Call Me Ishmael,*
Earthy Anecdote, Our Age Is Retrospective,
In the Ice Cream Parlor, It Is a Truth
Universally Acknowledged.
This was a silly exercise, but it got me
looking back at books I loved or wrote
or thought about. When I returned to Genesis,

it was late and I had been sitting too long
on my former lover's tall stool, bent over
his high drafting table. My body ached.

If you, as I on that night, didn't yet know
about consecutive preterite, you also might
sit too long on a tall stool wondering
how your education could have omitted the fact
that in biblical Hebrew, what God actually says
is, "Let there be light and let there be light."

5.

The six of us were each amazed
by different kinds of things. One girl found
the Aqedah so interesting, it made her think
all denominations' ministers-in-training
should have to learn Hebrew, too.
I heartily agreed from my plastic seat.
The room was either humid or freezing
depending on who took charge of the air.
That summer I was so stressed out
I had pain in my neck, back, feet, and teeth.
Sometimes I brought a tennis ball
to keep between my hip and the back
of my seat, to try to loosen something.
The Aqedah, said my classmate, was interesting
because if you didn't read Hebrew
you wouldn't see how many times the word
wood was used. Abraham cuts the wood,
takes the wood, lays the wood on Isaac.
Isaac sees the wood and fire, but no lamb
for the sacrifice. God will provide, says Abraham,
laying the wood in order and Isaac on the altar
on the wood. I liked that she was interested
in the recurrence of a single word. Adjusting

my tennis ball, which had moved, I asked,
Why is *wood* so interesting?
Because, she said gently, in my tradition,
this is a story that prefigures something.

6.

We were women. We often brought cookies
to share, chips or candy, coconut-coated
almonds sent from the South by a mom.
One three-day weekend resulted in a freshly baked pie
the extra day had allowed the crust of to rise
or set, I'm not sure. I didn't bake what I brought.
I drove my former lover's silver minivan
to pick up visitors. The rearview mirror
had fallen off shortly after I'd dropped him
at the station, though he'd spent the ride trying
to stick it back on. I was his subletter and he
a carpenter musician divinity scholar
on his way to collaborate in Sweden.

We'd met one night long before
when I'd slept at his feet on the threshing room floor.
I'd been advised to remove his shoes, then let him
tell me what to do. Bring me your coat.
He filled it with barley. Then one of us
went into the city. Later, he suggested we
"hang sometime" while we passed each other
on Market Street. He didn't stop walking,
only slowed. He told me he'd given
me barley because he'd never before seen me,
a rare quality, obscurity, in such a small town.
But you are my kinsman, I protested.
No, he said, I know your kinsman,
and if it's still true in the morning
that your kinsman will not do his part,

then I will do for you the part of a kinsman.
But I rose before one could know another.
What would he have given had he known me?

7.

The minivan was full of gear, the seats
lowered to make room. I wore sunglasses
I found in the car and listened to the musician
whose CD was in the player. He sang in a way
that annoyed, then addicted me. Aside from offering
no way to see behind me, the car seemed safe.
I drove it to physical therapy.

My therapist was Julia. She drove her thumbs
into my fascia. Julia, I said, it still hurts.
Are my ribs too splayed when I lean to the wall
to stretch my calf? Is my arm in the right place
when I bring the tension band across my hip?
And what about this, I said, rocking my ankles
over half a foam roller, am I doing it? I had questions
pain wouldn't abate. I rolled my foot
on a frozen water bottle, did shoulder releases
guided by free internet videos, and, in supportive shoes,
I walked to class with a stack of notecards
memorizing vocabulary for each day's quiz.
I learned words for *father, son, fire, mother,*
a word for *sheep, goats,* or *sheep and goats,*
words for *Solomon, Isaac, Moses.*
Some words I didn't learn, like *ghost.*
I was the best student in the class.
It was genetic, I joked. No one laughed.
I got perfect grades, higher, even, than A's
because of the curve and extra credit.
I walked past the same besuited
probable-lawyer every day

walking his handsome brown dog.
The dog's coat rippled in the already
swollen early morning summer sun.
What will you give now that you know me?

8.

Sometimes my former lover came home
from upstate New York or Sweden
and thought about staying on the couch
then stayed with friends. It would have been weird
in the morning. I hardly remembered his body,
only that something had soured between us
when I disinvited him from a poetry reading.
I told him readings were stressful
workplace environments for me.
We never recovered, though he fixed my bike
and I brought him three formal letters of apology.

V.

Apology

You believed they weren't real

Christians, so that if anyone asked you about them,
you'd give the etymology of the word

Evangelical, from the Latin,
to argue what it means

is not what it meant.
Etymology the lowest

form of theory, the shallowest
invocation of history:

Who cares what a word meant
if what it means now is different?

Just because the word meant that before
doesn't mean it means that anymore

even if you want it to,
which you do.

This was another difference
between us, that you loved and trusted

the past, believing it
should be restored, as if there were such a thing

as original meaning
whereas I loved the past

as the past.
I wanted you

to consider Christianity's bloody history.
You told me poetry's had been bloody, too.

Of the forced conversion of Jews
you cited Paul and said no one forced him.

I believed those you called fake
were the religion's logical and truest conclusion,

that in order to be Christian you'd have to reckon
with the idea that something endemic, structural,

facilitates an ignorance widespread
and willful and ask yourself

who you want to be.
We got in trouble visiting your family.

You must have known on some level
not to share my bed.

GODS PLAN in Scrabble tiles,
framed photos of teenagers mid-baptism

on the wall. I wanted you
to roll your eyes, too.

What about this is different
from a bar mitzvah? you asked me.

Purity. Everything.

New Angle

At your parents' your daughter
cut angels out of paper plates.

Angels have paper wings so they can fly
up to God, but no one believes in that
god anymore. Now god is
whatever Blake said.

What would an updated angel look like?
Someone screaming TREAT ME BETTER

The angels stood on their own
each in a side stretch, a play on grace
asymptotes make, the beautiful approach
that follows a line it will neither reach
nor run parallel to, and the new angels
don't laugh, they encourage you.

Parable

We went again, episcopal

A handful populated the pews, we
The only couple. You know it's a good movie

When everyone is there alone

After some singing from which I abstained
The priest spoke about loneliness

How on this, the day of His birth
God gave us Jesus to see us, how his first words

Must have been mommy and daddy
But his first Words were how is it that you sought me

You should have known I'd be in my Father's house

We talked about your gifts for your daughter
You'd done a bad job and I was angry

You'd failed her, the way you so often fail others
Giving them what you think they need

Not what they want. You wanted to work
At a soup kitchen on Christmas, to give

To the stranger. I'll go once you learn
To give to your daughter, obviously

A stranger to you

You'd read in the newspaper
What happens when someone receives a bad gift

It's that you don't feel seen, you told me
A bad gift is bad because it leaves you lonely

So Jesus was God's gift to us, the priest
Concluded his homily

New History

Maybe the worst thing about American Puritanism is the position it
forces its opponents into. —ROBERT HASS

I.

Jimmy, when we say sorry, is it I love you in disguise?
Everyone does it, marries the
Stranger, taboo to do it otherwise. When we say we don't
Understand, is it I could put my faith in you,
Someone I don't really know?

Compared to us
He was a
Rabbi. One thing
I want to make clear: these are my prayers. I don't
Say them to him, but against him,
The way your child leaned against my chest.

2.

Jubilant is how I felt when I fell for my
Equal, and not, finally,
Someone too old or too dumb for me. As the
Uvula to the throat we are
Shape note singing,

Collaborators in
Harmony. I was
Replacing my speaker when
I met you, at Best Buy,
Seeking to amplify that which lies beyond
Thought. You were what I bought.

3.

Joking, you said, you must be joking. I said I saw an
Eagle on the roof, some kind of omen related to the
Seeing of all things from above and what
Unity could such a vision provide? Spend how you want the
Sixtyish years you have left of your life, you said. You
Could spend them with me but you'd
Have to choose to. I said I could spend them even more
Righteously: celibate, in prayer, but still
It wouldn't be to your god. If you're going to blame
Sex for this discord, don't
Tell me. Tell it to the priest behind the grate.

4.

Justice I seek I attribute to
Envy: I want what I don't
See in myself, feel myself
Undeniably to be. Justice sees me
Slipping between my wish and my reality
Calm as a person who knows
How to sleep, keeping her
Right eye closed while her left, her left
Interprets the ceiling, which, too, is a myth, or so says C.
S. Lewis. I'm mostly just jealous of you,
Truth, whom so many men have devoted their lives to.

5.

Just came to see if I could, without mentioning you, if
Even a small pocket remained you had not infiltrated,
Swore not to touch, on the grave of your Jewish mother who outlived you.
Unbeknownst to us, we were the small split one
Side grew large from, so large it made me think a thing
Created to withstand doubt is built less to last than make
Hereditary. Ancestor, did we nourish you poorly? Why did you
Rise to spite us? We take care of our own. That's action, not an
Ideal. You died for something we won't let
Separate our
Tribe.

6.

Jessica is to be pitied, for she is among the
Elect who don't know this myth
Situated as fact in the womb of the one
Ultimatum god ever gave us: kill my son.
Sir, I'd have said, the boy is mine. Of course
We'd have to change the law to accommodate such
A father: he's otherwise the mother's faith if
Sired by her. What could we have done to prevent this? Finish what
Abraham started, the wood, no ram, and Isaac dead? We'd be
Just as bad, justifying the present by recasting the past. Oh,
Entertain us for a little while, god, before the
Weather burns or freezes, tell us a

7.

Juicy story about the birth of history, a boy
Evil is not the point of, how to fall, temptation
Snaking up our legs, pants to which apples are secondary, how you
Unstuck yourself from eternity that time you
Snuck inside a womb, where women take

Crude time and make a life of it,
Halving their own, leaving such
Residue as must be measured
In religion, half-lives, Judaism's
Shining drawer of radium, reserved for
Those who choose science instead.

8.

January: before I met you, I had not heard
Enough to judge. I'd only
Seen the highway billboards warning
Unbelievers of imminent accident, read
Salinger for whom you are a sage like any other,
Complete with thorny, convoluted text. What kind of
Hero goes around proclaiming divine parenthood?
Ridiculous as Icarus, Phaeton
In the Lookingglass production of *Metamorphoses*
Struts the stage like the
Teenager of a celebrity: "My father this" "My father that."

9.

Judgmental, judicious, joy-denying, as
Easy to hate as desire, is it even love if it
Stripes your uniform? My
Uterus could have carried any one of you
Slippery sons of god,
Could have delivered any one of you
Headstrong heliotrope hufflepuffers who know all
Relationships are with the mother and
Intuit precisely when to be born on a
Spinning planet that has been waiting for you
To put your finger on it, as on a spinning top.

10.

Jamba Juice still makes the mango one
Elizabeth and I used to get, a
Smoothie and a cheese pretzel with it
Until this proved antagonistic to our young life's project: being
Skinny, what our culture
Calls disordered eating, unless something
Holy comes of it—then it's called fasting:
Rainforest preservation, prophecy, genius (measured
Intellectually), atonement, Gandhi, prisoners released,
Simone Weil. Such a smoothie would be
Too sweet for me now.

11.

Jazz and classical, Joni and Taylor, Springsteen and the
E Street Band, August Wilson, Wyatt, musicals and plants
Share this: soul. Yes, it is its own genre, I know, but
Under whose reign was it yanked clean of governing policy,
Set between mountain and desert, in a
Correlation of height and dust? Who said
Human life began at all, let alone that
Reproduction requires conception?
It's one big line we
Stand in, goes back and ahead farther than we can
Tell. We don't know our place.

12.

Juggling, the blur of the balls, tells the arc of
Eternal motion, but these are no longer my prayers.
Save yourself. I
Unbraid from you completely, but so
Slowly it takes a lifelong motion
Capture video to prove I moved my

Hair a strand. There's no
Replacement for color now that all
Is gray and white. It's the end of our life.
Sing a closing song for me and I'll
Teach you to live forever.

13.

Jenny light, Jenny darkness: James Wright
Enjoyed writing by some personal candle that
Shone in his brain. What I love about James,
Underneath the certainty preexisting admiration
Shapes opinion into, is the way his poems
Civilize the dead—"I don't blame you"—life a
Heat love can be expended like, finite, with no
Return, or can, as an activity,
Increase the meaning of energy, the way a particle
Signals the presence of a wave. I love any action
That makes me stay.

14.

Jimmy, I love you. Do I tell you
Enough? I love your frown over a
Stupid book of philosophy, how
Unprepared you were to meet me, how I
Surprise you with your own laugh. If I were yours, I'd be
Constant, light as the cost of divorce is
Heavy. Let me cover your
Retainer. Blame me.
Invite me to dinner.
Spell my name in Hebrew letters. Give me a
Thorough tour. Me, outsider no more.

15.

Just when you thought it was
Ending, everything began. The
Sun rose upon the infected
Ur-planet, still arguably green and blue from
Space. Shadows cast by the
Central fire clothe our
Home, so deep in earth, a
Retiring form beloved of the
Insolent, inside which we
Sit like radiance,
Tutored by light, still learning.

16.

Journeymen and the rest of us teach
Ease to the
Sufferers out there laboring
Unduly, who have mistaken
Strain for work, authority for power, information for wisdom,
Confused dudes who bumble
Haphazardly from one concern to the next,
Reeling from false
Insight the way a child goes down a
Slide. One trains instead for a netless
Tennis match, resulting in that most desirable score.

17.

What happens in Wimbledon stays in Wimbledon. Lasting
Attachments still must be made, just not to
Serena, nor to any particular outcome of her game.
Alternative histories abet the passage of time, which
Juts out ahead, predicting, predicting. On that
Everyone places a bet, jealous of the future
Winner, insistent that it cannot be all.

18.

Juniper makes gin as
Elephants make ivory as
Silkworms make . . . duh.
Utility: "I belong," am of
Some use.

Collect my store into your
Harvest, take all I have a
Right to offer. Let me not offer what
I have no right to.
Spare my love from fear. Let him rejoice
                         Let him rejoice
His love is
Requited.
I have given it back.
Show me it was mine
To give.

Notes

"Numbers" is a contemporary rewriting of the author's d'var Torah from her 1999 bat mitzvah. "William James" borrows language from James's *Psychology: The Briefer Course*. "Paul Valéry" is a loose villanelle making use of a sentence Valéry used describe what is most boring about narrative writing. As a 2019 folio in the *Yale Review* put it, "The novelist's need to propel the plot, [Valéry] complained, frequently resulted in such mundane sentences as 'The Countess caught the 8 o'clock train.'" "New History" is an acrostic.

Some of the poems in this collection have previously appeared in the following publications: the *Yale Review* ("Berkeley Hills Living," "The Afterlife"); *Rainbow Agate* ("The Goner School"); *No Materialism* ("Numbers," "The Book"); *Aurochs* ("Homework Help"); the *Paris Review* ("Kings," "Consecutive Preterite"); *Annulet* ("Extra"); *Solar Journal* ("Thomas Jefferson," "Edward Thomas"); *Bennington Review* ("Admiration"); the *New York Review of Books* ("New Angle"); the *Drift* ("New History").

Acknowledgments

Thank you, Kōan Brink, Michael Dumanis, Zoë Hitzig, Christopher Janigian, Carlos Lara, Rob McLennan, Maggie Millner, Meghan O'Rourke, Jana Prikryl, Srikanth Reddy, Emily Stokes, Steve Williams, Grayson Wolf, and Alicia Wright—for your editorial brilliance and for publishing my work.

Thank you, Lisa Wells, Joshua Marie Wilkinson, Jude Wilkinson-Wells, Mark Levine, Jim McCoy, and the University of Iowa Press.

Thank you, Robert Hass, Katie Peterson, Margaret Ross, Rob Schlegel, Sara Deniz Akant, and the Exceedingly Merry Company: Jake Fournier, Dan Poppick, and Chris Schlegel. Thank you, Aria Aber, Jana Benitez, Sasha Debevec-McKenney, Eliot D'Silva, Leo Dunsker, Callie Garnett, Chloe Hall, Rachel Mannheimer, Jen Mazza, James Nati, Adrienne Raphel, Jared Robinson, Dana Swensen, Elisa Tamarkin, Noah Warren, The Mastheads, and the UC Berkeley English department.

Thank you, Joan and Gary Laser.

"Kings" is for Emily Davies and Abby May.

This book is for Ruthie.

Kuhl House Poets

CHRISTOPHER BOLIN
Anthem Speed

CHRISTOPHER BOLIN
Ascension Theory

CHRISTOPHER BOLIN
Form from Form

SHANE BOOK
All Black Everything

SHANE BOOK
Congotronic

ONI BUCHANAN
Must a Violence

ONI BUCHANAN
Time Being

MICHELE GLAZER
fretwork

MICHELE GLAZER
On Tact, & the Made Up World

DAVID MICAH GREENBERG
Planned Solstice

JEFF GRIFFIN
Lost and

HAJAR HUSSAINI
Disbound

JOHN ISLES
Ark

JOHN ISLES
Inverse Sky

JESSICA LASER
The Goner School

AARON MCCOLLOUGH
Rank

AARON MCCOLLOUGH
Salms

RANDALL POTTS
Trickster

BIN RAMKE
Airs, Waters, Places

BIN RAMKE
Matter

MICHELLE ROBINSON
The Life of a Hunter

VANESSA ROVETO
bodys

VANESSA ROVETO
a women

ROBYN SCHIFF
Revolver

ROBYN SCHIFF
Worth

SARAH V. SCHWEIG
Take Nothing with You

ROD SMITH
Deed

DONNA STONECIPHER
Transaction Histories

COLE SWENSEN
The Book of a Hundred Hands

COLE SWENSEN
Such Rich Hour

TONY TOST
Complex Sleep

PIMONE TRIPLETT
Supply Chain

NICK TWEMLOW
Attributed to the Harrow Painter

SUSAN WHEELER
Meme

EMILY WILSON
The Keep